ATIBA   CLAR

Unexpected   Words
from   a
GIFTED
AngeL

To the Villalon family,
I hope You enJoy
Much ♡

Atiba : ᵕ

ATIBA CLARKE

Unexpected Words from a GIFTED ANGEL

CoverdesignbyRtorMaghuyop
Interiordesignby Atiba Clarke

Published in the United States of America ISBN:

1978384101

1. Self-Help/Personal Growth/General
2. Self-Help/Personal Growth/Happiness
   13.07.19

ATIBA CLARKE

Unexpected Words from a

GIFTED AngeL

Dedication

I would like to dedicate this book to my family, friends, and anyone that is going through hard times in their lives and are trying to find a way out.

ATIBA CLARKE

Unexpected Words
from a

GIFTED
AngeL

Acknowledgment

First off, I would like to thank God for giving me the opportunity to write this book, because if it weren't for him none of this would be possible. I am truly grateful for what he has done. Sometimes when I'm in a situation, I forget that he is not against me, but he is with me at all times, and what I'm going through is a testimony for someone else. I would also like to thank a friend of mine, prophetess Edwards, who started some editing on this project; she is an amazing writer/ editor and one of the sweetest people I know. Finally, I would like to thank Tate Publishing and Enterprises for taking out the time for wanting to make this book come to life, and Ms. Ruth for giving me the idea to write this book. She has taught me what it takes to become a successful writer. But most importantly, a very big thank you for all the people who have been such great supporters of me since the day I was born.

Tips on What I Would Tell Someone If They Were Going Through This Too

1. **Never fight your battles. Let God fight for you (for those who believe in God).**

    Always remember to take the time out to pray and to have faith in whom we serve. But once you pray, you shouldn't have a worry in the world. If you do, that shows him that you lost your faith. So leave it upstairs because he will take care of it on his own time; you just have to be patient.

    Whenever I had a situation that came my way, I always used to stress and somewhat still do. But as I get older, the word *faith* becomes more clear to me every time I read Matthew 17:20 where it says, "Because of the littleness of your faith; for truly I say to you, if you have faith as a mustard seed, you shall say to this mountain, 'Move from here to there,' and it shall move; and nothing shall be impossible to you." I always try to keep that in mind because once I do that, God will bless me, and he will do the same for you.

2. Do something that makes you feel good.

It could be anything from listening to music, reading, going out for a walk, or watching a movie. Sometimes doing that thing you truly love will help you relax by keeping the mind and brain at ease.

In order for me to forget about what I'm going through, I either listen to Beyoncé, Ciara, or Christina Aguilera music or sometimes watch Ellen Degeneres, Smith family, and Tyler Perry movies. They all play one role in my life, and that is being a huge inspiration to me. I love them so much, and I hope I get to meet them some day. Every time I see one of them on television, I'm in another world forgetting that they can't hear me through the TV and that I sometimes have people in my house or on the phone (laugh out loud).

3. Never give up.

In life, there is always going to be something that will be difficult for you to accomplish. But that does not mean you should give up on it, because anything is possible once you put your mind to it. The only way you will be able to become successful at what you couldn't do before is to learn how to become—my favorite words that I came up with—a challenger agent. This is a noun, a person who's on a mission to look for multiple ways to score their goal: *determination*. So don't think it's wrong to fail because it's not, and you're only human.

I always told myself that before I reach the gates of heaven, I will no longer have cerebral palsy and will some day be able to walk on my own two feet. Don't get me wrong; there are days when I look around in my house and see photos of how I used to walk in my walker before I had all my sixteen operations, which caused me to become even more weak in my legs. Sometimes, seeing those photos makes me sad because I always say to myself, "If I didn't do those surgeries, I would still be in pain but still walking with a walker instead of using a chair. But I know once I keep on practicing every day, I will become a pro and will soon be able to walk on my own in God's time because he knows it's always been my dream. So just remember you've been put on this earth to accomplish not only the easy but the challenging times, and in order to get over the bridge, it must start with you.

4. Become a self-advocate.

You should never let anyone take advantage of you just because you are young, old, or born a certain way with or without a sickness. If you are not sure about something, it is very important that you ask so that way you will know for the next time how someone (individual or company) goes about proceeding with your request.

Remember that you have rights and that you are entitled to what is yours, so don't let anyone walk all over you or tell you something different. It is time for you to stand for what you've been working or worked so hard for even if it's something minor because it will, somewhere down the line, benefit you.

Another reason you should speak up is because when you are in an uncomfortable situation, the other person might not know how you are feeling. But whether you are dealing with important business or just a situation that has you feeling uneasy, you should approach nicely because you don't how they might react.

If you or a person you know has a problem with talking or writing, here are some tips that can help you or some else become an advocate. Have someone go with you to be your speaking advocate, such as a relative or friend who knows your situation.

Use a tape recorder to record what has been said; then have someone write down on a piece of a paper what has been recorded.

Before it was time for me to start my first semester of college, I took the time out to get familiar with the people in the disability office to see what services they provided. I had spoken with a lady who is the head supervisor of that office. I explained to her that I was interested in getting a scribe to write my notes from class and also for tests because it's hard for me to keep up with what the teacher is writing on the board while he or she is explaining something. Especially when it's time for testing I would never finish on time, so

I would use my extended time to make sure the test was completed. She said in order for me to receive services, I must get a doctor's letter and bring her my evaluation papers, so that's exactly what I did.

As soon as I got home, I called my doctor and told him my request and that I must have it before school starts. It was already the end of February and school was in a couple of weeks, but I still didn't have the letter yet, so instead of calling the doctor, I went to him and said, "Hi, good day. I'm here because I've been waiting since November for a paper to be filled out and a letter for school." The secretary looked in my chart and told me it still was not ready. I said, "You gotta be kidding me. I need this paper like today, today. School starts in a couple of weeks!"

She said, "I'll see if he could fill it out now. Would you be able to wait?"

I said, "It needs to get done. Even if I have to spend the night here, I will." So in the next five to ten minutes, she came back with everything in an envelope.

On the first day of classes, I went to the classroom expecting a scribe to be there, but no one showed up, so I used my tape recorder after ten minutes and started recording. Once class was finished, I went down to the office fired up because I was unaware that they couldn't find anyone for the whole week. I said, "Miss, I have carpel tunnel, and I've been writing all day because most of my classes won't let me use the tape recorder."

She said, "We are doing the best we can to find you someone, but in the meantime, try and get a classmate to copy your notes." I looked at her like she was crazy. I said to her, "I shouldn't have to bother anyone else who is on the same mission as me trying to become someone so they can have a better future. If you could find someone for my friends, then you can definitely find one for me. You are not going to take what I'm entitled to away just because I'm young and can't walk. God might have made me a little weak in the foot, but that doesn't mean I don't have a brain or mouth." I told them if I didn't have someone by the end of this week, I'm calling the board, but thank God I didn't have to because by the next forty-eight hours, I received a scribe.

5. Be proud of who you are. Everything has a purpose.

No matter where you come from or what you look like, it shouldn't matter because you should know that you are beautiful or handsome and special in your own way. You just have to find it deep within your soul, and you will find the uniqueness that was in you the whole time but didn't even bother to look. So turn on the inner light because it's ready to be seen.

Sometimes like when I want to go traveling there are some things that restrict me. Like for example if I wanted to go see my family in Trinidad and Tobago, I wouldn't be able to enjoy myself like I want to because of the fact that it is not wheelchair-accessible and especially when the roads are bumpy and narrow for an electric chair, which makes me sometimes question myself, "Why can't I be able-bodied so I can jump on a plane and go?" But when I finally get my life (laugh out loud), I realize that I am blessed because I'm alive and that I'm a miracle baby for a reason, which gives me a reason as to why I should be proud of who I am and never, ever question it. So become friends with that whatever reason of being proud of who you are.

6. Between a rock and heart place.

There is always going to be a point in life where we have to make the toughest decisions, whether you're a young teen, an adult, or maybe even for the sake of others. When it comes to making a decision, you have to put aside what you want and let God give you the answer because he knows what is best for you, and somewhere down the line, it will benefit you. As a parent, friend, relative, or spouse, I know sometimes it might be hard to make the right choice for your loved ones, but that doesn't mean you should beat yourself up for it. All you have to do is follow your heart, which means, in my opinion, that God is speaking to you to let you know that he's with you, but you must choose his path to guide you or your loved ones in the right direction. It is all about doing what's right because the outcome of that is a blessing coming your way.

When you are born a boy, it is common that at birth to get circumcised. Well, as for me, my mom decided not to get it done because being that I was so little with a physical condition, she felt that it was going to make my condition worse because of what the doctor was telling her. Thanks to them, years later, I started to have complications like constant itching and dead flakes. I had no idea why this was happening. All I knew was that those creams that I was using did not work. I was told by a specialist the reason why I was having those issues; was because of the foreskin, so by the age of twelve, I took the extra skin off. The aftereffect was horrible; I will never forget that pain, but as always, being sick didn't stop me. I hopped in my walker and went to school limping in pain without anyone seeing my facial expressions. Ever since then, my symptoms stopped, and my mother told herself to always follow her heart no matter what was being told by others.

7.   Power with two wrongs doesn't make a right.

If someone does something that makes you upset, try your hardest not to pay them any mind, because if you do, it will show how much power they have over you. When things get escalated, pull yourself away from the conflict. This will show how big of a person you are. Keep in mind that sitting there and arguing with whomever will result in being on the same level as they are. I'm not saying you shouldn't say how you feel because if you don't communicate, things will not be resolved, and from what I believe, not communicating is why problems occur. When it comes down to expressing what's on your mind, you must be stern, not nasty; it's very important you watch how you say it but mean what you say, because you have to be very mindful of the other person's feelings.

Just because that person got you upset and thought they have won doesn't mean they have won until you do what they did to you ten times worse. That's when you really show the power of their light bill going up because they know they have won by you getting upset and wanting to seek revenge, and by you doing that, you will get nothing out of it but paying the consequences. If you want good things to come your way, this is not the way to receive them. You can always seek revenge in ways like killing people with kindness, and when you do that, it does not mean you're stupid; it means you're one step ahead of the other and that you're thinking smart, because think about it, sooner or later that same person will be needing you for something.

I remember when I was in junior high school. My classmates always used to call me Chap Stick just because I used to put it on my lips every day, gay because of the way I used to talk or act around my friends, and even darkie because of my skin complexion. It used to really make me upset, and I used to give an answer back. One day, I was so mad that when one of them asked for a favor I gave them the "get out my face" look and silent treatment for months, and that's when the whole name-calling stopped. I know what you're thinking, "Why didn't I tell someone about this?" Well, I did; the only people who knew about it were the paraprofessionals and the teacher. I didn't want to tell my family; they would've come up to the school and caused a riot, especially my mother and sister, who will tell them to not even think about messing with me. They would have come up there and got up in your face just like Madea would, except the fact they don't have guns, wigs, or a big, old, blue dress. All they have are small-frame, nice-looking bodies with big mouths (laugh my a—off). So if something goes wrong, I try to keep the peace to my best ability because I know the family is not going to be around all the time to help me, and plus I don't want to have to bail nobody out (laugh out loud). But if it's something really serious, I make sure someone gets notified about it.

Don't get me wrong; there were times my anger would get the best of me and I wanted to serve revenge, but I knew if I did anything, it will reflect on my grades and what people thought of me. I never was that and never will be, and I always told myself that I would not change who I am because of someone. So think before you react because seeking revenge is not worth it, and at the end of the day, you and other(s) both lose. So If I were you, let them have all the fun while you get blessings coming your way for doing what's right because when you do that, all they're really doing is making you even stronger than you will ever be.

8. Moving on… forgiving and forgetting.

I know moving on might be hard because it's even hard for me, but whether someone hurt you or things don't work out in your favor, don't let whatever it is drag you down because there is more to life, and you should be grateful that you are alive and breathing and, most importantly, you are surrounded by your loved ones because that's all that matters. I have seen situations where people are in relationships for an amount of time and complain that things are still not working out after they have tried time after time to fix it but still stayed with the person. You shouldn't have to torture yourself to try to prove a point to everybody when it comes to your relationship. If it's not meant to be, why force it? Especially when you're not happy, you will be only making matters worse for not only you but the people around you. It's always good that you take notes on what your loved ones say because they just might be right; it's not all of the time they want to be in your business. It's because they love you and they want the best for you. This does not only apply for relationships as well.

It's always good to forgive because it shows you are being an adult about the matter. When forgiving, it all comes from the heart and how you send the message and tone to the other person(s). But if the person does forgive you, that doesn't mean they will forget. I know what you are thinking. You're thinking, "Well, what's the point of them forgiving if they won't forget" Well, in my opinion,   when they forgive you, they want to clear the air on the situation, but as for forgetting, it will be a task because they might be scared that the same thing might happen again. I'm not saying they won't forget eventually because you never know, but it all depends on where they stand with you and trust.

When someone does something to me, I take it to heart because I am very sensitive. I would be mad at my friends for weeks, and my friends would say, "Let it go already. You can't be mad at me forever." But I didn't give two cents; my motto was, "You shouldn't have done it. There should be no excuses." To this very day, I always wondered why things are the way they are with my father. I don't get to hear from him or see him as I would like to because he is a very busy man who lives in Trinidad and unable to come to the United States. But when I do hear from him, it's like the greatest feeling in the world because reaching out to him is a task. In 2011, I was able to get reconnected with him and my other siblings that I haven't seen since I was a baby. During the holiday, he flew me out to Trinidad, and I got a chance to reunite with him and my family that I didn't know. I stayed there for about two weeks. I had so much fun that I didn't want to come back home. Usually, I don't like to talk about my father, but I thought if I become more open about it, I know it will leave room for me to open up my heart more to him. The reason for that is because he is in and out my life, and it bothers me that he is not here to witness anything that I've been doing. I sometimes wish that he was here so he can really understand who I really am and what it's like to have a child who has a disability. My mother doesn't really like to talk about him, but when she does, it's what he has done. I try my best not to speak about him either because it will only make her upset.

The moment I realized that I decided to move on and forgive him for his actions was when I was accepted to go and see him even though I still didn't get the answers to my questions as to why things went down the way it did. I was really happy to see him after all those years, and I'm not worried because I know no matter what, he loves me in his own lil' way. But despite the fact that I may not understand all of it, I am truly grateful that God gave me the knowledge to understand that everything will be come clear to me one day and that I have a super mom to play both roles.

9. Temporarily.

In life, everyone has a story to tell because we all go through stuff; it's a part of life. But that doesn't mean we should let whatever it is take over our life. Sometimes, we forget that we are in this big hole for only a short period, and we must do what is right for not only you but for your loved ones, whether it's getting laid off or getting evicted, etcetera. It's important you act on it fast by having a backup plan. It's also important that you be grateful at the same time because it could have been worse; it all goes back to what I said in tip #6 about making a choice. So basically what I'm saying is that whatever choice that was hard to make before will not only benefit you but will only be for a little while, so just hang on tight.

If I had one wish, besides walking on my own and meeting my favorite celebs, it would be to get a job and move out of NYC public housing because having a motor chair living on the fourth floor when the elevator is broken prevents me from going out. Living in this apartment drives me nuts because some of the people like to violate the building, and on top of that, the apartment is small, and I feel like it has definitely outgrew us because my mother and I have been living here over fifteen years.

But like I said in tip #5, it's all about reasoning and accepting the facts about any situation, so sometimes when I get discouraged about it, I try to remind myself that living here is just temporary and at least I have a place to lay my head at night. I know that somewhere down the line God will bless me to get a beautiful house.

10. Speak the truth.

If you want people to respect you, it's always good to be honest. Once you tell a lie, it leads to a web of lies that will cause too much conflict for not only you but for others as well because you could be putting someone you love in danger. Lying will get you nowhere in life; it would make you look very foolish, which makes other people look at you differently and not want to be bothered. So if you are looking for forgiveness, just remember what I said in tip #8: the person may forgive you, but they will never forget.

I remember when I was about twelve years old and I used to date two girls at the same time. It was very stupid of me because those two girls were friends. I used to lie about being with only one person. I forgot how they both found out, but I will never forget how I almost peed on myself when they both ganged up on me. But thank God as we got older we were able to renew our friendship and keep the past behind us.

As a freshman in high school, I had a friend who became my stalker; she began to write me love letters, which I thought was kind of cute at first, but then it got worse. I started to get voicemails saying she loves me one minute, then get cursed out just because I wouldn't give her the time of day. But eventually, somewhere down the line, I ended up giving her a chance, which I know I am crazy for doing, but I believe everyone deserves a chance in life. And to be honest, what we had was kind of fun; we ended breaking up two months later because of a lot of things being said that caused bad air between us. Till this very day we do not speak as much; I chose not to speak to her unless she is over my friend's house and wanted to have small talk because just talking to her alone will cause even more issues for everyone. He wants us all to become friends, but I always tell him the reason why we don't talk is because of the lies she had told me. Yes, I know

I should move on, but how am I supposed to do that if there is going be no change in attitude? It makes it hard for me to open up my heart to trust anyone who took me for a ride. But no matter what happened, deep down inside at the end of the day, I truly care about her and want her to do well, and I know she wants the same for me. I am hoping that God removes the resentment that I am having and hope we become friends, because I realized that this is not moving on, and giving each other the power to get upset is not the key. So as you can see, me and moving on is something that I have to work on a little bit more. So speaking the truth will keep you out of problems, and it's very important you try your best to fix the issue by letting it heal and not torture yourself by trying to get the truth when it's not ready to be spoken, which means don't go looking for it; let it come looking for you because you don't wanna end up like me where I always used to try and force the truth out and still get the same answer. And what I learned is that by you doing that, it will show the person that you are upset, and so they will keep at it. But if you keep to yourself, sooner or later things will become clearer.

11. Talk it out.

I know sometimes expressing your feeling can be difficult at times no matter what the situation is, whether it's talking to someone you admire, talking to your parent, or talking about an issue that needs to be resolved. But in order to feel better about the matter and yourself, you and/or the other person must find a way to release the thoughts; you can either draw it out or write it out in a letter or have it in a journal for personal use; these methods should help your soul, and just remember when expressing, it doesn't mean you have to get loud and be ignorant because this will get you nowhere. But then again, we sometimes forget where we are, and we tend to lose control; it happens. :) Laugh out loud.

Being expressive with my family about my love life can be very awkward, especially with my mother; she always tried to get me to talk about when I am ready to have sex, and every time I say I plead the fifth, and then I object, laughing out loud. I guess because she is a woman and I'm the only boy in the house without a father, it makes it very weird even though she is doing a great job playing both roles. The people that are in my life know me as being very vocal when things are on my mind that I need to bring forth to someone, especially if I need to tell someone off, and you better believe they laugh their rib cages out (laugh out loud). But with all jokes aside, like I said before, we all have that something that's not easy to say, and as for me, that is telling my father about how I feel because he is not around. And I don't really know how he is going to take me and play the role of being a detective because he is definitely not the bonding type. Laugh out loud. Sometimes I ask myself, "Does he know who I truly am? Does he think about me? I wonder what it would be like spending time with him on a daily basis, etcetera." These are the questions I still have no answers to. I thought about asking him when I saw him, but something was holding me back, and in a way, I'm kind of glad because maybe it wasn't the right time God planned. I know when you're reading, you are probably wondering will I ever talk with him about it and how will I feel better about it. Well, as I am writing this book, it has made it easier for me to talk about it even though I talk about it with my mother; sometimes, it's much easier for me this way, and yes, hopefully one day I will be able to. I am hoping that God guides my lips like he always does to give me the words to say because I know it may look like I'm putting him on the spot, but that is not my motive. I just have to do this for me so I can grow healthy, not just physically but mentally.

12. Lessoned learned.

Life is a book. In order to make it, we must make mistakes in order to improve who we are on the inside; the only person who does not make any mistakes is God. If we make a mistake, it's okay because that's life and that's why he put us on earth to learn as we go. You are wasting your time if you sit there and beat your self up when you could be finding a way to fix it. People will not only respect you for not only doing something about it but owning up to it and learning from it.

From what my sister told me, there would be times where she would disrespect our mom, and when she finally moved out to Virgina with her friend, her friend told her how her mother would mistreat her and that she must not make a mistake of being disrespectful to our mom again, and that she should be thankful to have a parent because most kids don't have a relationship with them. My sister would always tell mom she loved her, but ever since her friend told her the story, she began to say I love you more than Barney (laugh out loud) because she realize that it could've been worse and she regrets being rude even if our mother was in the wrong. But I must say regardless of what my sister's friend went through, she refuses to let her mother's mistakes mess up who she is, and from what I can tell she is doing a great job at staying sweet and humble, and that's why I love her.

13. Facing your fears.

Being scared does not make you a punk; it only shows you have a sense of feeling and that you are being real with yourself, so don't feed in to people's stupid comments when all they're doing is teasing you about being a chicken or coward because you are not; you are so much more than that. You are so unpredictable that no one can touch you. The reason why overcoming your fear is so important is because you will receive the knowledge to know that you can defeat what your brain thinks is scary, but it's really not; you just have to tell yourself that it's like a goal so that way you can have motivation and courage to not only face your fears but to do other things that are safe and not damaging to your beautiful life. What really matters is that you prove overcoming your fear to no one else but yourself.

My family thinks I am fearless because of the things I have been through, but just because I look at the nurses taking my blood or getting injected in the mouth with no vaccine so many times doesn't mean that I am not scared of anything. I fear a lot of things, which are going under the knife, falling being under the influence to change who I am, and not ever be able to walk. When it comes down to anyone having surgery, it is normal for you to be nervous, but me on the other hand, I take the word *nervous* to another level. Laugh out loud. I start shaking, throwing up the morning of when there is absolutely nothing in my stomach, and once I start crying, everyone in my family starts crying. In order to keep me calm, I always ask the nurses to hold my hand and to have some music playing once I get inside. Laugh out loud.

Being that I am now learning to get back on my feet again after all these years, it's kind of scary sometimes doing all of these exercises that I haven't done since God knows when, like for example going up three flights of stairs had me petrified. But I knew if I let fear get in the way, there was no way I was going to ever accomplish my goal. I had to tell myself that if I ever want to walk again, I have to let go of my insecurities and face what I am up against. The second week into physical therapy, I found myself walking up the stairs like no tomorrow and wanting to do more, like balancing myself in front of the mirror and using the treadmill. I have always been the motivated type to want to, but it was something about that very day that made me feel my drive ten times more than what is was.

To make sure I stay in character, I stay prayerful no matter where I am, and just remembering my accomplishments and the great things that people say about me keeps me moving forward. The reason why not staying true to myself scares me is because watching and hearing the things that are going on in the world today, you never know who you are going to be tomorrow, so just be mindful of things around you and think about your future. My fear at this very moment will be writing this book because the thought of millions of people reading about your life and your feelings can be weird especially since it's my first. And my main concern was being to open and to approach the truth without regretting what I put on paper. But I realize in order to inspire others and get closer to my dreams, I must let go and let God. I know that he's guiding my hands on this keyboard to type every word I write.

14. Cherish.

When it comes down to having material things, it should be the last thing that matters; sure, you should appreciate everything you get, but what's most important is that you cherish your family because at the end of the day, that is all we have. I know sometimes they get on our nerves, but that's only because they love us and want the best for us. We must remember that we can choose our friends but not our family and that the days are not promised, so it's important that you cherish every moment that you have with them. It kills me to see how some kids/adults disrespect their parents like they forgot where they came from. I think most of that come from the source, which means that the reason why they could be acting like that is because of something that influenced them or it could be something in their past. The truth might not come all at once, but in order to get your answer, it's always better to take the person back to the incident to start the healing process and to see what can be done.

As we all know, it is normal for all family to go through their issues, and of course, my family and I don't see eye to eye. The people who argue the most are my mother and sister because they think and act just alike. I call them the Bopsy Twins. Laugh out loud. When they get together, they cannot be in a room for more than five minutes. Like for example, my mom is the type of person who is always in a rush no matter if we are on time. We are still getting ready, and she is over there with her little short, tiny self holding her drink walking back and forth like a little bee, yelling, "Let's go," and my sister will be like, "Yo chill out, son," and there my mother goes sucking her teeth, cursing, saying, "Y'all was supposed to been ready, and why the house look like that? What you been doing all day?" Then they go at it with each other.

Sometimes, I have to tell them to "get yo life" and have several seats—laugh out loud—especially my mom because she will be on twenty when she is supposed to be on at least um…zero? Laugh out loud. My mother and I don't really argue like we used to because she knows I am getting older, and she knows I will tell her what's on my mind. We don't really butt heads that much because I am more laid back and I think before I react; with her, it's a whole different story. She does the panic attack, then take something to sip on (laugh out loud). To make a long story short, for those who have seen Tasha Smith playing Angela in Tyler Perry's *Why Did I Get Married?*, that's whom my mom reminds me of. Laugh out loud.If we do argue, it will be mostly about money or keeping on my socks in the house, which I hate wearing. Sometimes, she makes me so mad that I want to just shake her up, but at the end of the day, we both love each other and we are still family.

15. Live your life.

Stress is known to be the #1 killer, and if you sit there worrying about your problems, what people have to say about you, and what is going on in their lives while they're focusing on being happy, all it's going to do is put you in the hospital. I have seen incidents where a person can't get over the person they like or they were with in the past, and they would do anything in there power to break up what's been done because either they are not happy with themselves or don't want to see anyone else strive for happiness. If you are or know someone who is going through this issue, let me break it done for you. You or that person need to have several seats (chill out) because there is no need for you to be upset with your past if you claim you are happy with the present. Stop looking back and stay focused on what you have in front of you and enjoy life to the fullest and don't worry about anything. It's all about having fun!

My name Atiba is an African name. It means understanding and wise, and a lot of people who know me say that's what I really am, but if you look it up, it also explains that I am considerate of others and can tend to worry about everything, which is very true. My family calls me Mr. Worrier because I get easily worried about anything I was born high risk (quick to go get in to a stroke). Ever since I was sent to the hospital for my minor ulcer and my panic attack, it became a wake-up call to reevaluate my life and, in any situation, to stay calm because being in bed at the hospital is not worth it, and I thank God he was able to teach me how by putting his hand on my shoulders.

16. Practice what you preach. Share your experiences.

It is not good to pretend that you have it all together, and you really don't; it's one thing when you own up to your issue and you're trying to fix it, but don't go telling other people how to live their life. If you're doing the exact same thing, it's always better to come together and share how we can help one another by talking about the same or the similar issue. You never know, just like how my advice is helping others, your words might be as powerful as mine.

I know their is always going to be a point in my life where things are going to be out of order, and that is why I respect myself because if I don't know something, I will admit that I have no knowledge about it whatsoever; for instance, math, science, and me do not get along (laugh out loud). My friends wanted me to help them with their geometry homework because they didn't understand it. So I said, "Let me take a look at it." Once I saw that paper I said, "Oh child (country accent), y'all better return to sender because I do not understand jack neither. I guess I'm going to have to hop on the boat with you guys (laugh out loud).

17. Promises/thingsaremeanttobebroken.

In life, we expect things to happen when we want them to, but sometimes we have to leave room for disappointment because if we don't, we won't be able to grow with independence. Sooner or later, we will eventually have to go out into the wild for ourselves and learn that we can't rely on people to do things for us. It might take awhile to learn the word independence, but once you hit that boiling point, you will finally get an idea.

For anyone who is a single parent or striving to make it through, you keep going because it's not about relying on something or someone in your life; it's about having a conversation with God and asking him to put his hands on you and give you that independence that you always had but never knew, and you better believe he will set you free from all the broken promises, whether it's a doctor giving you the run around or your baby mama or daddy leaving your child's hopes up for nothing.

Before my father got deported for multiple felonies, I used to always look forward to seeing him, but it was always some excuse, and I used to get disappointed. My family always knew not to promise me anything because I will nag them about it until it happens (laugh out loud). I thank God for getting me out that stage. Laugh out loud.

18. Smile.

No matter what you have going on, you should smile because you don't want to spread any bad vibes and bring other people down with you. You must learn to separate your issues between work, school, and home; otherwise, people wouldn't want to be around you. This is a thing called life; not everything in life is going to be a happy moment, but remember you have so much to look forward to.

People always tell me what makes me so special is that no matter what I'm going through, I am always smiling. I tell them it's because I know I have a purpose in life, and I am going to get to that purpose no matter if I get hit by a ton of bricks. All that matters is I have life, and whatever comes my way, I smile because I know it's God's test, and, regardless, I will get passed it.

19. Treat people the way you want to be treated.

Sometimes in life, we are all not going to get along, and that is completely normal, but if you have a problem with the whole world and don't have a reason why, you shouldn't take it out on others because your problem is not their issue. When dealing with others and communicating, you must have respect; otherwise, people will not respect you, and things will not get done in a timely matter. If you keep this up, people are not going to want to be bothered with you.

One thing about me is that I am respectful and stay to myself, but I don't let people walk all over me just because I'm in a wheelchair; I say what's on my mind and don't hold anything back. I mean, sometimes it can come across kind of mean, but I always make sure it makes people laugh at the same time. Because that's what people love. They say it's not what you say; it's how you say it, and they think of me as a comedian. If I'm not respectful, that means I don't have any respect for myself, and I know that I can't live like that because God is watching everything, and he will not bless me with what I want.

20. It's never too late.

No matter how old you are ,it's never too late to accomplish your dream by going to school because that's what's going to get you there; it's not about being a certain age. It's all about holding the key to your destiny and how many lives you can change. Being in the streets will not do anything but put you behind bars, and if you have all that time to be in the streets doing your dirty work, then you can put the same amount of time and knowledge in your books. Staying in school, work, etcetera will also show people not only intelligence but that you are a go-getter and no one can stop you because whatever it is, you will be the greatest at it.

After I finish everything with this book, my plans are to return back to school, but if God takes me and this book in a different direction, I shall go because I know sometimes what you think or plan to do isn't what he wants you to do. I thought I would be in school right now because writing this book was not my intention even though giving advice and helping others is what I love to do. I guess God saw how much of my heart and soul went into school that I forgot to take out for me and that it's okay to enjoy your life too.

21. Ask questions/back up yourself.

If you are unsure of something, it's always good to ask what's on your mind. You will be smart for asking but a fool for not knowing because the more you know, the smarter you are. It's also important because wherever you go or what you do, you want to make sure you have some type of confirmation to be reassured.

Anything that I do, I make sure I ask questions till I can't ask no more (laugh out loud) and have some type of document that says what's been said, and if I don't understand, you better believe I will be calling or in my chair on the bus on my way to your office. Laugh out loud.

22. Set a deadline for your goal.

If you want to make it to a certain point in your life and you want to fulfill your dream, you must first start to have a positive outlook on life; then you must jot down your goal and your finish line date and start gathering ideas on how you think it can happen if you're lost for ideas. Then ask around; this is how you build your circle. Once you have your support team, you must make sure you keep looking at that paper you wrote on every day to remind yourself that you cannot back out and time is running out. When you finally make it, make sure to give back to the world; those people were the ones who bent their back for you to reach this day.

If it wasn't for wish coordinator, I wouldn't be here writing this book. She has been so kind trying to help me grant my wish to meet Beyoncé. I had gotten so discouraged and ran out of ideas, and she gave me this suggestion, and she said that if I needed any advice, I should not hesitate at all to ask because we all need a helping hand. My goal is to not only help others but to make my dream come true at the same time and be able to give her a copy of this book myself. No matter how many no's I have been given, I will not quit as long as I already got a yes from God. Till this very day, I am still working on my wish and definitely make it to the finish line.

23. Do the best you can.

Nobody is asking you to beat yourself up and be a perfectionist; we all have issues in a certain area. All you can do is try and move on. You have to look at it as you put your effort into something that might benefit you in the long run, and it's for a good cause. So lose those bundle of nerves and have fun with what you're doing because that's what it is all about.

Besides me having trouble walking, I have trouble putting on my shoes and in the process of learning how to but as for cooking, I'll just leave that to my mother. Laugh out loud. But other than that, I am independent. I dress myself, go out, etcetera. My mother is so blessed that she doesn't know how blessed she is; she still thinks of me as of her baby, and I know all mothers do, but when I don't try to help myself, it's the end of the world. Laugh out loud.

24. Stay on top of things.

Remembering might not be easy because you have so much on your plate, but if you don't have your priorities straight, it can cause issues with what you have to get done. It's always good to have a planner or phone book to write down the time, day, and the person's name to keep track because you will soon learn the word *adult*, and no one will be able to keep track of your stuff but yourself.

I am known for having a photostatic memory; I can remember people's phone numbers, passwords, etcetera. Some of my friends including my mother forget their passwords, and I always have to remind them. Yes, it's that bad. Laugh out loud. If I forget, it will have to be in the moment, and I would have to get sidetracked by something.

25. Stop feeling sorry for yourself.

There is no reason why what you want to do should stop you just because you might have limitations. It's all about telling your mindset that you are human and it's okay to feel down sometimes, but you can't let it control your whole life because if you do, you will be missing the wonderful opportunities that are out in the world. Please don't let it pass you by.

I thank God that he was able to guide my mind to not want me to be spoon-fed because it could have been much worse. People always tell me when I speak, they don't see me as being in a wheelchair because my mind is so sharp, and the things I say show how mature I am about life. I don't let being in a chair stop me. I make sure that I live my life and have something to do like go to movies and concerts, go swimming and traveling, etcetera. Every time you turn, I am always in the street either hanging out by myself or with someone. My family always says I go out more than they do. Laugh out loud.

26. Love something enough to let it go.

Sometimes we have that one thing that is so hard to get rid of, whether it's someone or something that you love because it's been around us for so long that we got so used to it, but if you don't learn to let go wherever you stand, it might be harmful toward you or anyone around you, which you might be aware of but don't want to do anything about or it could be just that you don't know how to. But when it's like that, you must pay attention; it can mess up your growth, mental state, family, and friends.

One of the hardest things I ever had to let go was my dear friend Ms. Betty. She was not only a home attendant to me. She was also like a grandmother to me. I love her with all my heart. She began working for me at the age of nine, and ever since then, she became a member of the family. This wonderful lady has been working with me for about eight years. Letting her go because of her health was the hardest thing I have ever done because throughout the years, she taught some valuable lessons about life. I had to accept that she wasn't going to work for me anymore, and if she continued to, she wouldn't be any good for me, less alone for herself.

27. Responsibility of issues.

the more you sit there and worry about other people, the less you will get done for yourself, and the more you juggle other people's issues, it can lead you into depression; you will not be able to please everybody. If you want to help, the best you can do is show your support and give suggestions; it's up to the person to want to take your advice because it's their life, not yours. They are going to live it the way they want to live it.

Whenever someone has an issue, I'll be more than happy to give them advice. My family and friends call me Mr. Counselor because I am always giving some piece of advice, and as I do it, I try my best to stay mutual because it's the best way to go.

28. Embracing.

Owning up to your problems can sometimes be embarrassing, but we are human. If we don't experience these natural causes, we wouldn't be normal. These things are what make life. So whatever you find that you don't like about yourself on the outside, just work with what you receive.

A lot of people call me skinny and boney; But I don't pay them any mind because at the end of the day I know I look good (laugh out loud). No one has to tell me. It's also good to embrace your health problems, believe it or not, because it will show that you have courage and strength to feel better about yourself, and the more you do that, the more confidence you will have. A couple of months back, I was diagnosed with mild anxiety problems and was on meds for a month, which I am not ashamed to say because it's a normal thing that happens to everyone. Thanks to only taking the pill for that amount of time, my anxiety problems went away. I learned to embrace this issue by going to see a counselor because this is something I feel I need help with, and I have no problem saying that.

29. Never wish bad on anyone.

If someone has done something to you, it's never good to wish bad on them because it can happen to you, and when it does, you will not like it. I mean, we all come to a point when we all feel like strangling the person, but deep down inside, we don't want to do that because we love them. All we can is let them fly on their own until things resolve and wish them the best in their success.

Whether or not I get into it with someone, I never wish bad on anyone; the most I would do is be mad at you and won't want anything to do with you until you come clean. But don't get me wrong, if I did something, I will admit that I was in the wrong and that I was pretending it didn't bother me, but it really did. I mean, don't we all sometimes find ourselves doing that? You might not want to admit it, but it's the truth.

30. Evaluate around your world.

Too much negativity is no good if you have people you come across that just try to bring you down. That means they want what you have and don't know how to access it and that it can happen if they will be supportive; it's just a matter of when because everyone has their own calling time. But if they have a hard time understanding what being a supportive team means, then you have to reevaluate the people in your circle because that means they never wanted to see you succeed deep down in their heart but just pretended to be happy for you until something major happens, and then they start showing their true colors.

That's one thing about my family and friends; no matter what I do, they always back me up, and I know it's because of the love we have for one another. I love to interact with people, and very family-orientated, I will make sure to support in any way I can.

31. Get familiar with your surroundings (just in case).

Becoming independent can sometimes be a good thing, especially when it comes down to traveling. You want to make sure that you or your child knows where to go and who to contact because you never know what might pop up in the last minute.

When I go out I like to take the city bus even though I have a car, which I know it does not makes any sense, but I like to feel independent. I hate the feeling of being underneath my mom 24-7. Now if I have to go somewhere far, it's without doubt I'll use the car, but if she is not around, I use my last option—a transportation service called NYC Transit's Access-A-Ride. I called them stress-a-ride because they are so unreliable (laugh out loud). They come late, say they were there but really wasn't, and they even expect the drivers to pick up the next person two to five minutes after you were picked up, so I try not to use them that much unless I really have to. But as you can tell, I get around and if something happens I am always on my feet, knowing what to do and how to go about it.

32. Do what's right in spite of.

Killing people with your kindness doesn't mean you are weak; it means that you are showing maturity and who you are as a person because sooner or later, that same person who was treating you like crap will eventually need you for something, and you know what? Go ahead and do it; it may sound stupid, but you are not because you will receive many, many blessings.

Some of my friends think I am way to kind and want me to treat others the way they treat me. But I can't live like that. That's not who I am. If I do what has been done, how am I supposed to receive my blessing? At the end of the day, nobody wins.

33. Say what you mean, and mean what you say.

Being contradictive can start a lot of problems especially when it comes to friendships and dealing with business, because whatever has been said before, that person is going to take your word. It's not good to go back to what you said five minutes ago and say you never said it. People are not going deal with you because they don't know which way to go or come with you and take you as a complete joke, so make sure whatever you do, be stern and mean business.

Ever since I was young, I would always make sure things were in place because I am not the type to go back and forth when it comes to organizing or taking care of my personal needs, like doctor's appointments, going out, etcetera. Even though my mom is around, I taught myself how to become a young gentleman.

34. There is a time and place for everything.

Causing a scene will not get you anywhere, but the crazy thing is that you are not hurting anyone but yourself, and you might think people are laughing with you. But the truth is they are laughing at you. All it's going to do is make you look stupid. If you have to address something to someone, it's always good to pull them a side, and if they don't want to listen and instead want to act like fools, then that is their business; you did your part, and the rest is unwritten.

As you can tell, I love my mother dearly, but she takes me there sometimes. We could be going out and she is over there cursing in a rush to go nowhere 95 percent of the time. I don't pay her any mind, and the other 5 percent, I admit I can't help but want her to shut up (laugh out loud) because the things that come out of her mouth are really not worth anybody's time, and what makes it so funny is that she knows that she is in the wrong but doesn't own up to it. We could have been to where we needed to go, but instead we are arguing like two dumb fools in the middle of the street because I'm trying to get her to understand my point of view, but if it's not how she feels, then oh well (laugh out loud).

35. Become a leader, not a follower.

If you have someone who you look up to in your life, it's important to follow in their footsteps because they obviously want you to succeed and go down in the right path just like they have; it might take a little while for them to understand what life really is about, but they did it. So make sure to leave a mark where you are.

I know a lot of people who got caught up doing the wrong things, and my sister was one them, but she finally understood that she's falling down the wrong path by hanging with the wrong people who were doing illegal things, but eventually decided to become a US veteran at the Navy. Even though she has three kids, she still found a way to travel around the country for years and months and still be there for them. I think of her as being like a second or third mother because every since I was a baby, she always used to be the one to wake me up and get me dressed while my mother wasn't around. Whether she was going down the wrong path, she will never show or tell me or her kids what was going on.

I truly honor and respect her for who she is, and watching her succeed makes me feel like a proud parent who doesn't even plan to have kids yet (laugh out loud).

36. Becoming dependent.

Having money, drinking, and smoking will not solve any of your problems; all it's going to do is keep you numb for the time being, but it's not really making you happy as you may think. The only reason why you turn to all these things is because you might feel that's the only thing you can depend on, but it's not. These things do not make up life; they only ruin it, and if you want to live for a long time, this is not the way to go. If you're not good in handling your issues, don't be afraid to seek help because we all need it, and sometimes our feelings can be all bottled up and we wouldn't know.

Just because I struggled with my health in the past couple of years, I still didn't depend on those things. I chose to keep my head clear by finishing school and doing what's right, because if I didn't my life would've been haywire whether I used a wheel or not. But I am now in college and writing my own book. Don't get me wrong. I might still have my issues, but I do look at the bright side. Ever since these panic attacks started happening, I waited a little while before I went to the doctor, but it had gotten to the point where my heart was beating out my chest, and I told myself I don't care what anyone says. I am going to seek help, and so I was put on medication, which by the way my family couldn't stand— they felt I was going to one day become dependent on it. But for once in their life, they didn't have to force me to take anything. And out of all the times when something was finally helping me, they want to fuss about it (laugh out loud). I would tell them they might be my blood, but they were not in my body. I know how I feel. You cannot tell me how I will be feeling today, next week, or next year (laugh out loud).

37. Don't let it get away.

If something comes your way, that is your chance to grab it and run; don't wait for it to disappear, and what I mean by that is if you are in a relationship or received a special offer, don't let your past interfere with your future because you deserve some type of happiness in your life, no matter how much hurt you have been through.

Everyone wants to know when am I going to start dating. To tell you the truth, I don't know. My mindset isn't fully ready for that as of yet. But then again, sometimes it can get a little lonely. It's like I want it but don't want it because I honestly have to say it might have a lot to with me not having a lot of trust in people and letting people in because of my last relationship. But once I get back in to school, I would probably open up my heart in the love department (laugh out loud).

38. Grass isn't always green on the other side.

If you have someone or something good in your life, it's important to hold onto that because what you think you might get in the other outlet might not be what you expected, and not everything you get in life is fully 100 percent. It always happens like this; you got the 80 on one side and the 20 on the other and end up complaining about the 80, when it's usually the better half and go for the 20. But somewhere down the line, you find out that the 20 wasn't what you thought it was and want to go back. But sometimes, when you go back, you still end up losing because the 80 finally moved on, so just remember to be grateful for what God hands you.

Whatever passes my way, I am and will be always grateful my family have always known for me not to be a fussy person. When it comes down to asking for stuff, I'm not really that guy. If I do ask, it will be mostly to buy concert tickets or get stuff that I really need not so much want maybe once in a while. My family does most of the giving and sometimes buying, and if they don't buy, I do it myself because I know what catches my eye.

39. Remember where you came from.

Sometimes when we finally receive our blessing, we end up getting caught up in what's not really important and forget that we came from the bottom and worked our way to the top. Everyone has to work hard for what they receive because everything doesn't come easy. Whether you have a billion trophies, awards, or bucks, your family and the people around you were the ones who got you to where you are now, so make sure you treat them like you always have treated them—because all the glamorous stuff is not what made you who you are today.

My family and friends told me once I become famous, I better not forget them, and I promised them I won't, but my friends on the other hand, they want me to sign a contract saying that I must stop whatever I am doing to pick up the phone (laugh out loud). To be honest, I am scared because I just hope it won't change my image and hope I stay the same because watching what happens in the entertainment business makes me think about how people twist your life story around, and it's not even true, and it makes them go crazy. But in order for my mindset not to change, I am going to trace back my steps on how long it took me to write this book and what I am going to accomplish during the time. My other goal is to give back to anyone in need who has and will be supporting me in anything I do.

40. Don't procrastinate.

The longer you take to do whatever it is you need to do, it will never get done on time; things don't get done by themselves. The only way things can get done when you need it is when you do it yourself; it is always better that way anyway because waiting on someone to do you a favor will take a million years, and besides, you know how you want things to get done.

I am not going to lie. I really wanted to back out on writing this book because my computer broke, and I had to write by hand; then my physical therapist ended up giving me a USB mouse and keyboard to finish working, but eventually I got my new laptop.

I told myself that I can't give up because I already committed to doing it, and people were patiently waiting, and I know what I'm doing will help others, and I will also be making my dreams come true as well. Writing has never been my thing until I started high school, thanks to my English teachers. I had my lazy moments when writing this book; sometimes I say to myself, "Man, why did I put myself through this and keep pushing it off ?" But I kept putting my mind frame by just imaging me on *Oprah* or *Ellen* and saying that it will happen, so I kept pushing those buttons on my laptop (laugh out loud).

41. Don't discuss your business with everyone.

If you tell everyone what's going on in your life, then people will spread it, and the whole world will know and take what they see or hear and take it to be more then what it is, and sometimes it could just be you having issues with a friend, boyfriend/girlfriend, or spouse, and you ended up telling a family member or friend, but then a week later, you end up talking to them like nothing happened. And that still won't stop your family member or friend from being extremely mad not only at them but at you for doing what you thought was right. So please make sure to think twice before telling your whole life story for the news to report (laugh out loud).

Most people think of me as a private man because I don't like discussing my business with everyone. If I do discuss my business, it has to be with a certain person that might be going through the same issue or if it's something that's going to benefit me in the long run. Most of my friends confide in me when they have an issue going on because they know I won't say anything. I am so personal about what I do that everyone calls me the businessman because of the way I handle it. I taught myself how to become a man and to depend on no one when it comes to certain things even though my family is around. I know eventually they are not going to be, so I taught myself from early.

42. You made your bed, now lie in it.

It is nobody's fault that you created a mess for yourself or whomever; make sure whatever you do, you fix it because you're the who started the problems, and no one will be able to help you but yourself. No one wants to get caught up in a mess, so before you want to start trouble, think twice because you might not want to clean it up.

Every now and then, everyone likes to hear a piece of drama because it can sometimes be entertaining. I know I do (laugh out loud). And then again, too much of it can be annoying. When it comes to causing issues, I'm not the one. According to the critics, I'm a counselor (laugh out loud). By you starting trouble, you are the one who is being a child; it's time to grow up and get yourself together.

43. Can't have your cake and eat it too.

Everything in life is not for you. If things don't go your way, then it doesn't give you the right to be nasty to anyone. Usually, when that happens, it is because someone in their life has spoiled them and gave them everything they wanted. The way life is made is where we must work for our wants; otherwise, we won't understand what the meaning of how it is to be successful. I think being spoon-fed is a curse because when it comes to dealing with certain things, you will have no respect for it not unless it has something to do with you.

When it comes to giving in our case, my mother and I, love to give, but the difference is when my mother does not get her way; it's like World War I and II unfinished (laugh out loud) because you will never hear the end of it. She starts huffing and puffing like the bad wolf, sucking her teeth like the straw is trying to get the ice to break in a Slurpee, and makes the sound of a truck when it stops (laugh out loud). Everyone in the family calls her crazy because her mouth is just on the loose; she gets on our nerves, but we love her. As for me, I don't like to share with my mother when it comes to food or money; sometimes, I don't know why (laugh out loud), but it's something I'm working on.

44. Don't jump to conclusions.

Assuming can cause you issues with others and with yourself; people will not want to talk with you because they sense a lot of trust issues and doubt. You are only making yourself look crazy by doing that, no one else.

When I was younger, assuming was one of my biggest issues. A lot of people used to get upset over it, and my friends and I would get into arguments. But after a while as I got older, I noticed that habit disappeared by seeing what happens to other people.

45. Runaway.

From your issues does you more harm than good because sooner or later, they will catch up to you and can become much worse than they were before and will somewhere down the line give you bad results.

As much as I would like to avoid certain situations, it's impossible. I have no choice but to face any giving situation that presents itself, otherwise if I don't it would make me less of a man.

46. Start protesting.

If something has been taken away from you or your community, you have the right to start a riot but in a good way. It's important to have a support group so that they can help you come up with some great ideas like putting up posters, speaking out loud at press conferences, making videos, etcetera. People might think you are wasting your time on things like this, but you really are not because that one little small thing can turn into something really big.

Yes, being disabled or sick can be tough, especially when you get your benefits taken away for God knows how long, like SSI, food stamps, or home care. Once these things get cut off, you have to start a whole process all over again, and sometimes it can take weeks, months, or years. Being that I have home care services, every year they have a form that needs to be filled out before thirty days, and if not they are not filled out, your services will be cut, and it happened to me because my doctor was taking to long to fill it out, and it took me about eight months to get my services back on. After a while, my mother and I began to call every day, and we eventually got it.

47. Look back.

Sooner or later, we will be able to laugh at our issues, which is a good thing because laughter is medicine and will make you feel better when it comes to having a clear mind.

Sometimes, I say to myself, "What was I worried about? If I have my faith in God, I should have laughed about it." It's the way through the misery because I know that he will lift me up and take me higher from whatever it is, and I bet you feel the same way after your situations.

48. Take constructive criticism.

When doing something that you love for the first time, it's always good to take people's opinion on what you did, so that for the future you know how to go about it because whatever was being said was not to hurt you, it was to make you better.

I hope when this book comes out, I get as much feedback as possible good or bad because this is going to help me build up my career and show me how to please my fans in anyway I can. In writing this book, I learned that there was no point in turning back; my life is out and it's not going to be about me anymore.

49. Mark the day.

On the day you complete your goal, it's always good to write down the day your started and the day you achieved your goal so that way you can celebrate your success; it doesn't matter how you go about it even if you have to walk out side or light a candle.

Once this book is completed and released, I am probably going to save up some money to go to the spa to massage my brain (laugh out loud). I started this book in June 2012 and finished in February 2013. I can't describe the feeling I was having when I finished it. I felt like doing flips (laugh out loud).

I hope my words of wisdom can help you with whatever it is that you are experiencing. Please take every word I was writing and cherish it because I wanted to make sure I have given you my heart and soul. I look forward to hearing from you and can't wait for you to meet me and read more of my upcoming books.

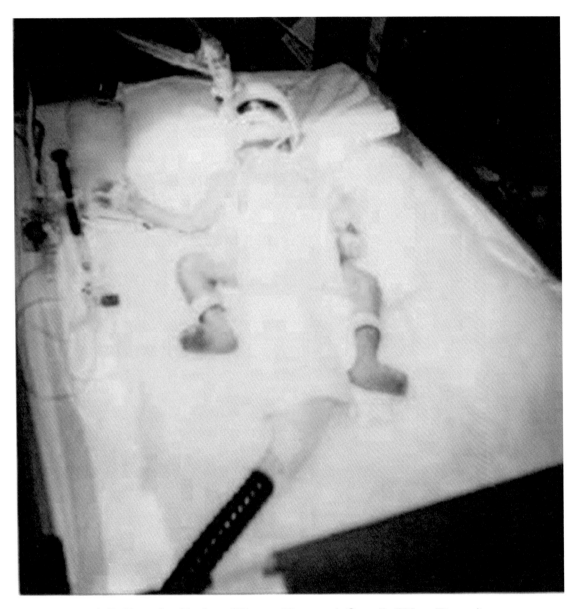

A Miracle Baby (Two Days After I Was Born)

The lovely nurses.

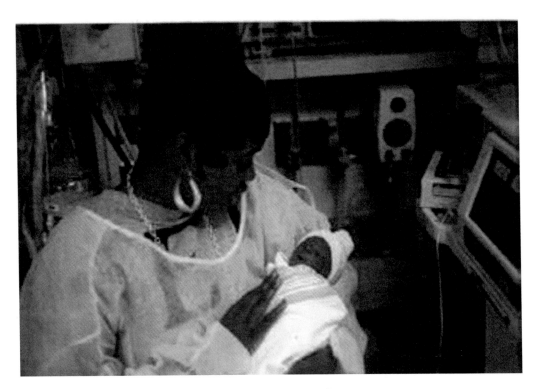

Momma's baby boy

At my christening ceremony

At my christening party

Home therapy

I'm busy running around and playing with my toy.

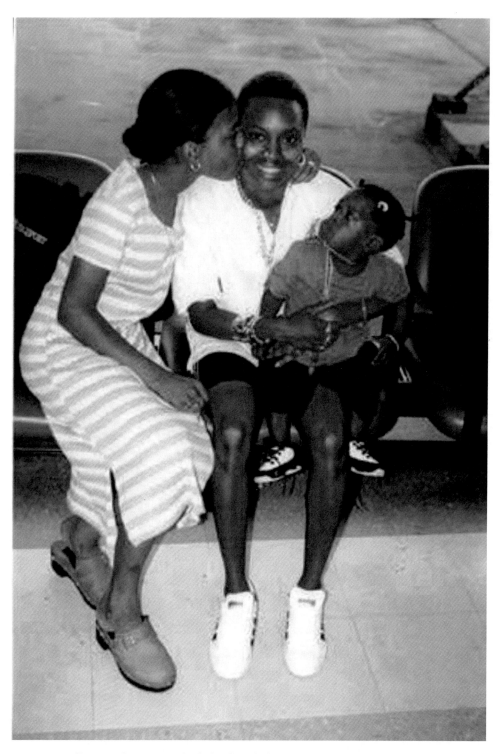

My first trip to Trinidad with my mother and sister.
I was looking at my sister as if I didn't know her
and wondering why she was kissing my mom.

My mother and I at my pre-school graduation.

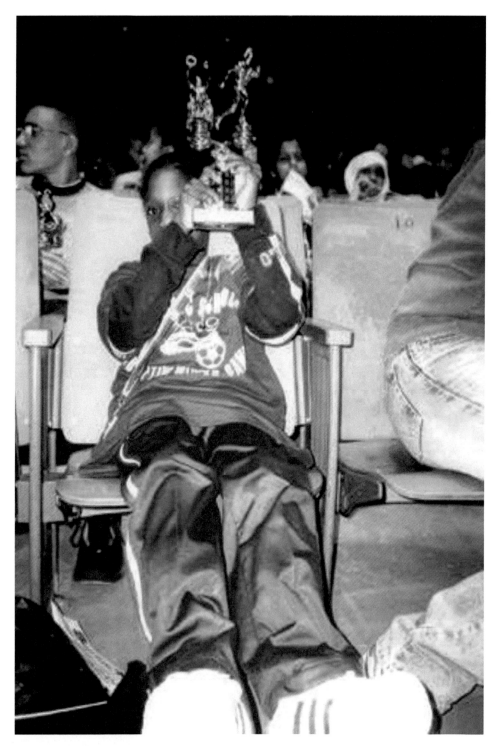

This is me at the special olympics. I'll always be a winner!

I was only six and people were already
calling me speedy gonzoles

We were always smiling. Pictured are my
best friends Mikey and   Jonathan.

I was always cheering people on. Pictured are
my best friends Penny and Matthew.

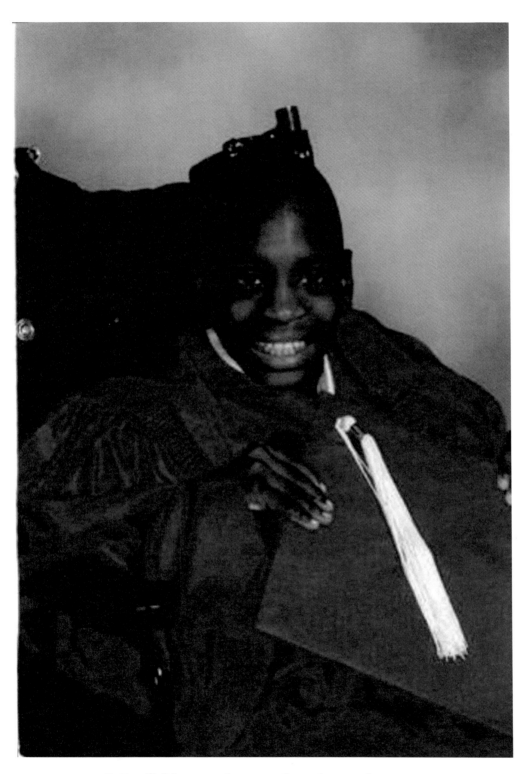

My fifth grade graduation picture.

Heading off my 5th grade prom but before I go
I must give mom a kiss (Laugh Out Loud)

5th Grade Teacher Mrs Smith

Excuse me while I make my entrance into my
junior high school prom.

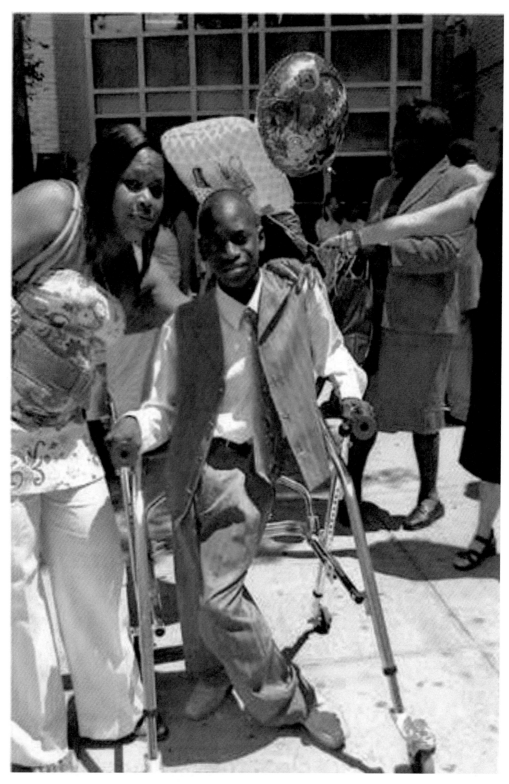

My Aunt Hazel who I love very, very much.

Proud sister
(My J.H.S Graduation)

I love you Ms. M. Thanks for   everything.

My Little Munchkins Amari, Ashe, Akahji Even Tho
they Can Get On My Nerves I love Them Very Much

Looking Swanky For My H.S Prom

The Best Day of My Life Graduating H.S

H.S Diploma

Mr Lodico H.S Principal

My Aunty and Cousin Amanda Clarke

My 18th Birthday

She is Always Making Me Laugh Love you!!

My Autobiography

Good day, everyone, since you've had the wonderful opportunity to read inspired words I would now like to share my experiences with you on why I wrote this book. Well, throughout my whole life, my family and friends always told me that despite what I've been through, I am one of the most influential, self-motivated, and sweetest people they know. On June 28, 1993, I was born with cerebral palsy (CP) as a premature baby weighing in at 2 lbs, 3 oz, at Brooklyn's Long Island College Hospital. Right after I was born, I was put in the incubator and hooked up to a machine for about two months.

My mother, Ms. Curline Clarke, who was born in Trinidad and Tobago, decided that before she had any kids, she would move to the United States with the rest of my family members for a better life. My sister, Adanna Clarke, who is also from Brooklyn and older than me, has three adorable kids. She and our mother would come every single day with or without the rest of the family to visit me and cry their eyes out, not just because they were worried but because I made it into the world.

Before you knew it, two months arrived and I was out the hospital. The doctor advised that I start some physical therapy in order to gain more strength in my legs so my condition wouldn't worsen. While I lived in the Bronx, New York, I received therapy at home for the next couple of years until it was time to move to Brooklyn, New York. My mother felt that the Bronx wasn't the right place for my sister and her newborn boy, especially given my condition.

By the time I turned two, I was starting to learn how to walk with a walker and embrace the experience of preschool at United Cerebral Palsy (UCP). In the months after I started school, my mother realized that my eyes were very unusual, so she immediately took me to the eye doctor. He confirmed that I was cross-eyed, and in order to fix it, I would have to have a procedure. So my mother agreed and scheduled the next appointment. I must say that the doctor was absolutely right. In two weeks, I was able to return back to school with brand-new eyes. In the year of 98, I began elementary school at PS 222.

Those five years were the best years ever. Because of that school, I was able to define who I was becoming and what I wanted to be. I remember the time where I was given the opportunity to sing in shows, write a two-paged speech to be read over the loudspeaker, and race at the Special Olympics

To win awards. My mother always used to tell me how she never understood how a child like me loved school so much. Going home at the end of the day would be so sad, and I was always looking forward to the next morning. You would think when I got sick I would want to stay home, right? Nope. I told myself that I must pass my classes and that is exactly what I got on my report card, passing grades.

In the middle of my senior year, I started to develop a change in my walking. Every time I would take a step, I would walk on my tippy-toes and drag my feet. My doctor explained that I would have to undergo a two-hour surgery to strengthen my muscle and that I would have to stay home for six weeks. I was really disappointed. On the day of the operation, one of my baby teeth was hurting, so I had to go get it taken out before the surgery could proceed. I was so shaken up, but I was so happy that my family was by my side. After I woke up, I was crying my eyes out because the healing process was torture. By the end of the fourth week, I called my doctor and told him that being home was driving me insane, and I would really like to go back to school. He told me that it was okay for me to go back. When I got back, I was so behind in work, but being that I was so tired, I was unable to complete it all. My mother wrote a letter saying that I was in pain and I couldn't finish my work, so my teacher approved and told me I can hand in my work any time; it was fine with her. But I gave her most of it anyway. She only needed two

Pages from the packet, which I started when I got home but again couldn't finish. Just because of that, I got detention the next day because she was in a bad mood.

Even though my last year was not the best, it was really sad to know that the time had come for me to leave the place where I took my first steps, learned my ABCs and 123s. That upcoming fall in the year of 2004, I entered the halls of Shell Bank IS 14. I loved it their but not as much as PS 222. Things were great in my life until the beginning of my senior year. I started feeling pain in my hip every time I would walk, so I took a trip to the doctor's office, and he ordered numerous tests that all resulted negative. He prescribed me some painkillers and sent me home and assured my mother and me that it was nothing, but my heart told me otherwise. I still went home and did what I was told. No matter what I did, the pain never went away. I kept going back to the doctor. After a while, he started to think I was making it up because every single test would come back negative. One day, I came up with a solution to have me admitted in the hospital to run a series of tests, and that's exactly what he Did.

During my stay, none of the other tests came out positive, so I had asked my doctor if I can do the MRI again because something just didn't feel right. I knew something was wrong, and I wasn't leaving that bed until I got the answer I needed to hear. Sure enough, I got the results back, and it showed that my hip was partially out of the socket. I was so relieved

That I had finally got my diagnosis and proved to my doctor that I was not crazy. My mother and I were told that I would have to do a five-hour operation that consisted of putting a metal plate in my right hip, which will make my legs uneven and that I would no longer be growing. The answer to how all this happened to me is still unknown to this very day. Even though school was about to start, I had no choice but to do the surgery.

The day finally came, and my stomach was doing flips when it was time to go in. Right after I woke up, my back started to itch, my eyes wouldn't open, and I couldn't breathe for my life, and all I could hear was my mother and home attendant scream, "Nurse!" The next thing I knew I was knocked out again with Benadryl.

Right after I woke up again, I was greeted by a nurse who told me that I had an allergic reaction to the pain medication penicillin. She took my vital signs and transported me up to my room. A couple of hours later, my doctor came upstairs to make sure that everything was all right with me. He showed my mother and me what he had done to my legs. He put a big blue sponge with straps that were strapped around my ankles so that when I am sleeping, my legs wouldn't cross, but as for my hip, it was stapled down with a patch and taped. When my mother saw that, her skin began to crawl. My doctor said if I felt any better, I could go home the next day and that I must have more hours from my home care service for help and that my next follow-up appointment would be in six weeks. As I was getting discharged the next day, the nurses went over the instructions and meds. They made sure that I understood what was being read, including that the big blue sponge was *not* to be taken off.

By the time I got home, it was nighttime, and I was in so much pain. The sponge was between my legs and made it really difficult for me to sleep. Every ten minutes, I would doze off and go right back to sleep and wake up again. Sitting upright was the only way I was able to sleep. All I kept thinking was, "These next six weeks are going to be torture!"

The next morning, my home attendant arrived, and the first thing I asked her to do was to take the sponge off because I couldn't take it anymore. It was just so uncomfortable that what my doctor said went right out the window. When my mom woke up, she came straight to my room and noticed that the sponge was no longer between my legs. She immediately started to scream at me. That is what she does when she gets nervous (laugh out loud). As she was calling my doctor to tell him that I took the sponge off, all I could hear was her sucking her teeth and huffing and puffing, like a sanitation truck that stops to load the garbage (laugh out loud).

Once my mom got the approval that it was all right to take it off until I got ready to go to sleep, she started to calm her nerves, and I was so happy to know that I could stretch my legs out without straps being around my ankles. Several days later, the pain started to go away, but that didn't mean I was completely better. I started to have stomach pains, trouble going to the lavatory, and lack of appetite. I felt so miserable, my mother and family tried everything in their power to get me to drink prune juice, eat bananas, and even get out the bed and wheel around with the recliner chair. But my answer was always either, "That's not going to work," or a flat out no. I know they were only trying to help me. But I just didn't want to be bothered. I was in pain and my butt was sore from sitting. This made me really annoyed because I was restricted from bending my knees.

So I had to remain with my legs straight out, and no matter which way I tried to turn, it was still uncomfortable. All I could think about was the work that I was going to miss from school. Two weeks later, I was finally able to use the bathroom by drinking milk of magnesia. I felt like a woman who was in labor for days and finally got to get some sense of relief. Boy was I happy (laugh out loud)!

Before you knew it, the day finally came for me to follow up with my doctor. He said that I was healing up great and would be able to return to school the next day. This meant I got to take the bandage and staples out and even go back to crawling (that's how I get around in my house). In order for me to start back walking, he said I must continue physical therapy and follow up with him in six months.

As soon as I got home, I got out of my recliner chair and got down on my hands and knees, without even remembering that I was supposed to be bedridden for at least a month with my legs straight out. I don't know what I was thinking, it hurt so bad that I was crying like someone had died. The next day, I went to school. Even though I started my senior year off a little bit late, I was still excited to know that I was graduating. I was so grateful that I didn't miss much and would be able to hand the work in that I missed on time.

The following week I was scheduled to take my graduation photo, and it was one of the happiest moments of my life. Before it was time for me to take my photo, my para and I were on a mission to fix my afro. It was so nappy that she had to throw water on it in order to comb it. I will never forget we only had ten minutes to run to the bathroom and then rush downstairs. As she was pushing me, it felt like we were shopping on black friday (laugh out loud), but thank God I made it on time.

A few weeks later, I was out the recliner chair and in physical therapy trying to get back into the groove of walking again with my walker. Doing an exercise was one of the hardest things I have tried to fulfill because my legs were straight out for a month without moving it, and that made my muscles cramp up. The pain was terrible. I would cry my eyes out while I would try to do the exercises. I knew that the devil was trying to come after me because two months before my graduation, I started to feel pain in my hip again. So I went back to the doctor and was told he had to reopen my leg because the plate he put in was rubbing against my skin. If I didn't take it out, my cerebral palsy could have gotten worse. Once the same day, surgery was completed. I was discharged and able to return to school the next day.

I returned to school after so many interruptions, with my head up high and not realizing that I still had an 84.2 average as well as people who loved me because of my kind spirit no matter what hit me. They were really amazed at how quickly I would jump up from being knocked down, and thanks to the grace of God, on June 22, 2007, I was called a graduate from Shell Bank IS 14. I would never forget how my family was crying like the *Titanic* was sinking and how I received a standing ovation while walking toward the end of the stage. I just couldn't believe that in three months I would be roaming the halls of Edward R. Murrow HS. Once I started, things were all right until the middle of spring. I started to feel pain in my right knee every time I walked. I waited for about two weeks to see if the pain would die down, but no luck.

So I went to my doctor, and he reminded me that when he put the metal plate under the bone, it caused my right leg to be shorter than my left. He told me in order to get my legs even, I could either wear a lift in my right shoe or put pins in my left leg to see if my right leg would catch up. But if that didn't work, I could cut some of the bone in my left to make it look exactly like my right. My doctor said, "The bad part is that the surgery will keep you in bed for at least eight weeks, and you will have severe pain." As soon as those words came out of his mouth, he immediately got a straight no about the eight weeks recovery time. I told him that I would try wearing the lift shoe because going under the knife again was the last thing on my mind. At that point in time, my mother was helpless because she hated to see her child in such pain, so she would just go along with my decisions after awhile.

By the next two months, I got the shoe. I hated it because the right side was big and ugly, while the other shoe was regular. I felt like I was a clown about to do a circus act (laugh out loud). My mother would always yell at me about not wearing the shoe, and when she did that, I just ignored her (laugh out loud). Several weeks later, I'd decided to suck it up and go ahead putting the bolts in my knee. I kept it in for about a year because the metal was scraping my knee just like it was doing when it was inside my hip. Shortly after that, I began to feel severe pain in my hand, and I had no idea what it was. The pain was indescribable. I did everything including the one thing I really hate, taking meds, and everybody knows for me to take meds, I must be in pain. So of course when I went to the doctor and was told that all my tests came out negative, he said it could possibly be carpal tunnel syndrome (CTS), but to be sure, I had to take a special test called an EMG. He said being that I crawl a lot and use an electric chair that could be the reason why. Two weeks later, the results of the test came out positive. He gave me a brace that didn't help me at all, and this left me with no choice but to go back under the knife. However, the outcome made me feel like a little kid who's excited about opening their gifts on Christmas (laugh out loud).

Before you knew it, I was out of my sophomore year and entering my junior. Those were the worst two years of my life because I was always sick. Everything I drank or ate would come up. I would have serious migraines. Whatever I would do to try to get rid of the pains, nothing would work. So I went the ER and I was told that my stool was backed up, and that's why I was having these pains. In order for me to get rid of it, I must drink Mirolax.

A month later, I developed a new symptom. Every time I would urinate, I would feel a burning sensation. The first thing my mom asked me was whether I was sexually active. I looked at her like she was crazy (laugh out loud). When I arrived back in the hospital, they finally decided to admit me so they could run some tests, but of course, a positive result was a no show!

My doctor began to think that I was making it up or that I could be stressing. In a way, he was right about stress probably causing my sickness, but as for me making it up, he was way off. I am not the kind of person who would lie about being in pain. So after a couple of days, I got discharged, and so I notified my school that I would be returning back the next day. I knew it was very foolish of me to return so soon, but I was already behind, and plus I really love school. No matter how sick I was, I would push myself to go. My friends, family, and teachers would ask me what I was doing in school when I was so sick.

One day I was so sick that I couldn't even keep my eyes open. My body felt like someone hit me with a bat, but that didn't stop me from going to school that morning. As I was pulling up my jeans, my mother was fussing at me while she was holding a plastic bag to my face because I was puking up my life. After school, my mother took me straight back to the hospital. My doctor admitted me again and called in a gastroenterologist who was really nice. She checked me out from head to toe and advised that I have an endoscopy. The result from that procedure showed that I had gastritis. She explained that when she was observing the inside of my stomach, the lining was red and irritated from all the medications that I've been taking while I was recovering from the all of the surgeries. I was so grateful to finally have the real answer and not being looked at like I was a chicken with its head cut off. As I was being discharged, she prescribed some acid pills, and ever since then, my stomach pain vanished and is no longer a battle of mine till this very day.

When I returned back to school, I received my report card with all passing grades except one.My math teacher who was a very cool guy had no choice but to fail me because he didn't have enough work from me. This was true, so I couldn't argue with him. If I wanted to graduate the following year, I had absolutely no choice but to makeup the class in summer school. You and I know I didn't want to be there any longer than I needed to be. So thanks to the grace of God, I passed and was able to become a senior.

Usually, if you're a senior, it's supposed to be your best year of life, right? Well, not mine because I had reached the graduation requirement, which consists of you needing 44 credits, and I had 45.8 but still taking electives due to budget cuts in some classes. But on June 24, 2012, I received my high school diploma. I was so excited about starting college because I knew I stepped closer to fulfilling my dream to be a psychologist or a nurse.

Two weeks before I was supposed to start school, I was reading the Bible and looking in my closet and came across the big, ugly left shoe that I hated wearing. God said to me, "If you want to get back in your walker again, you must change your mind about cutting some of the bone off your left leg so that both of your legs will be the same length. I know that the eight weeks of recovery might seem long, but if you trust me, you should know that you will be okay." I will never forget those words he put in my heart. So I went ahead with the surgery. I had never, ever, ever felt such a pain like that in my life. It felt like someone was ripping my skin.

For a second, I thought again I was a woman who was in labor about to give birth (laugh out loud). I told myself that this was the last surgery I was going to have. But the good news is that I no longer had to stay in bed for eight weeks, only three, because I was healing very fast, and it turned out that having the surgery was a good decision because both legs were now even.

The day before I went to take my bandages off, a visiting nurse came to see me. She woke me up out my sleep to take my pressure, which was fine, but my pulse was 130. She had the nerve to ask me why it was so high. I said, "Miss, you woke me up out my deep sleep. What do you expect?"

She said, "Well, if I come back, and it's still high, I'm sending you back to the hospital."

I said, "By you telling me that, I'm going be more nervous." So she left and came back, and it was still high, which meant I had to go back to the hospital. As soon as I got there, the staff did an EKG and CAT scan. I wasn't feeling sick until I got to the hospital, and all because of that dumb nurse, I ended up staying overnight and missing my appointment because they wanted to make sure I didn't have anything on my lungs. Thank God the prediction was wrong. The following week, I went to take off my bandage. During the spring of March 2012, I started my first semester of college and passed my classes, and in the middle of going to school, I returned back to physical therapy and I'm now back on my walker.

I am so grateful for what God has done for me despite of what I've been through because I know he only made me go through all this stuff so that I can share my testimony with you to let you know that you are not alone. Whatever you go through, it's only temporary. You must keep in mind that whatever doesn't kill you will only make you 100 percent stronger. I always told myself that no matter what I was going through, I was never going to lose hope because I have life that needs to be cherished to the fullest, and I have dreams to accomplish. It's important you do the same by dreaming famously and reminding yourself that if I give up, I'm not going to be known in the light of who I am. Taking off from classes to write this book has been such a fun experience. I leaned so much about myself, and I hope you enjoyed reading this as much as I enjoyed writing it.

Made in the USA
Lexington, KY
20 June 2018